DOMINATING OIL PAINTING: A
Complete Aide for Craftsmen, everything
being equal

Corey Mitchell

Table of Contents

CHAPTER ONE

INTRODUCTION

Oil paint is a totally thrilling medium to work with. One won't anytime become drained while painting with oil paints. There are various materials and different mediums expeditiously open and when you set these materials and mediums with the versatility of oil paints, you have different spellbinding ways to deal with starting an oil painting. There are sure drawing and painting mediums that are commonsense with oil paints and when used, will make your masterpiece experience genuinely interesting and boggling.

CHARCOAL

Charcoal works wonderfully as a vital stage to oil painting. There are three vital sorts of charcoal utilized most frequently by masters and they are full, willow and plant charcoal. Willow and Plant charcoal will much of the time be significantly more exceptionally enjoyed for starter drawings as they make a lighter etching and are less challenging to delete. Compacted charcoal, since it leaves a lot hazier line, is more challenging to discard and not as broadly used to begin an oil painting. Several consistent contraptions to use for working with charcoal are controlled erasers, firm fiber brushes, blenders and tortillions. Anything that sort of charcoal drawing you make, make certain not to overdo it with your application. Charcoal is extremely forgiving with oil paints, however as far as possible, and it can influence the paint in irksome ways.

PAINTING ON A FORMED GROUND

Subject to the sort of particular picture you are pursuing, on occasion the white of the material can be preposterously unbelievable or have a lot of detachment which makes beginning a work of art rather badly designed. Utilizing a uniform formed ground on your help, will make it significantly more direct to denounce the qualities in your association. You are permitted to utilize any grouping you like to condition your material. A piece of the more prominent tones are warm reds, yellow and regular tones. Forming your material is straight forward and will not need that much time. First make a flimsy wash utilizing Yellow Ochre and Consume Umber. Apply the wash to your help liberally. Utilize a colossal fiber brush to completely spread and cover the help. Award the wash to dry for a couple of moments and sometime later clear off the overabundance with a surface. You don't need to utilize oils to condition your material. You can condition your material with any of the water mediums portrayed under.

ACRYLIC PAINT

Acrylic paint is a prominent decision for beginning an oil painting and one of my top picks. One of the most captivating parts of acrylic paint is its fast drying time. This property of acrylic paint makes destroying in you're under painting exceptionally essential. Examinations can be worked out rapidly on your material and well really of accepting that your under painting will dry, you are prepared to paint in not more than minutes. This truly relies on the kind of acrylic paint you are utilizing and how thickly you apply it. Despite the way that the quick drying is time drawing in, however as in other water based mediums, there is persuading clarification need to thin the paint with risky substances like turpentine.

WATER DISSOLVABLE PENCILS

Water dissolvable pencils give an astounding technique for starting an oil painting basically in view of their versatility. The significance of this medium is that when dry, it behaves like a conventional covered pencil, yet when water is added, it extraordinarily imitates the properties of water tone. This empowers the master to both portray point by point limits as well as make wonderful washes.

WATER DISSOLVABLE OIL PAINT

Different gifted specialists are not that acquainted with this last medium like a general amateur to the universe of painting. Enter, water dissolvable oil paint. With ordinary oil paints, a standard framework for beginning a show-stopper is by crippling the oil paint with turpentine to apply washes. The issue with turpentine is it's an unimaginably perilous substance. Different specialists develop forebodingly weak responses to this substance and can't utilize it. The significance of water dissolvable oil paints is that no turpentine or other harming substances are required. They can be reduced with standard water. Once more water dissolvable oil paints act a ton of like customary oil paints and your brushes can be cleaned with cleaning specialist and water, keeping away from the need to utilize horrendous designed compounds.

CHAPTER TWO

MOST EMINENT WORK OF ART OF THE BEST IN CLASS TIMES

Oil painting is a particular sort of painting where drying oil is applied as paints. Never-ending assets of verbalizations, oil works of art down the ages are visual documentations of the plan of experiences culture and way of life of the ancient times. With the moving patterns of all that working out continuous examples and procedures have made a way into the designs making them more improved and versatile. Oil Painting is moreover truly outstanding in the general times. The cutting edge specialists and epicureans esteem them and advance novel thoughts from them. Different sorts of oil were utilized to make oil creative signs. Linseed oil, poppy seed oil, sunflower oil and pecan oil were utilized generally. The painters blended the oils in with the assortments with remarkable expertise and precision. Pine pitches and frankincense were applied to welcome a reflexive impact on the show-stoppers. Generally speaking the associations were cut on a material. Anyway, every so often the expressive arts were worked out in paper sheets, cardboards, flooring and wooden sheets. Creature paste and gesso were utilized to cover the board materials. Current gesso is a mix of calcium carbonate and polymer acrylic. It is utilized to develop the softness of the establishment layer of an oil painting. Creature stick saves from the risky horrendous impact of the paints. In oil show-stoppers the outline of the subject of a specific association is first eliminated on the material. Then, at that point, colors are blended in with oils to plan shades of arrangements. Colors having cobalt, manganese and lead were utilized in days of yore to develop the drying structure. The oil tones are then applied on created by craftsmanship as layers. With the presence of oil painting tubes the painters have been liberated from the dangers of blending oil in with colors. Painting in layers is the customary system for oil painting. This is finished to refresh the impact of arrangements and convey perfection into the inventive creation. First the "under painting" is portrayed out utilizing precarious layers of paints like the turpentine paint. The layer is left to disappear. After this two or three layers of oil paints are applied sequentially letting each layer to disseminate totally prior to applying the going with layer. It can call for a short investment to months to dry an oil painting totally. After the work is fixed by the master stain is applied to bring the shining impact. There are many spellbinding genuine factors and terms that you really want to be aware, quite a bit early, about oil painting in the event that you hope to take it up as an unwinding development. By knowing these terms, you will truly have to get an overwhelming comprehension of oil painting and become a specialist about the nuances attracted with that sort of painting.

You, above all else, genuinely need to get a handle on what the terms worth and collection temperature mean. In expressive arts, you genuinely care about to make the progress of the varieties from a dull variety to the light tone. Esteem is the term that is added to this change from dim to light that is made in the compositions. By making changes in the worth in oil painting, you will be capable get a superior difference in your composition. One more term connected with oil painting that you might not have heard before is variety temperature. Variety temperature is only the put of a variety on a variety wheel. By utilizing the variety wheel, finding out about the cool and warm colors is conceivable. While the warm ones have a rosy color, the cool ones are found to have a somewhat blue color in them.

Oil painting can be delegated long and short oil paints. These assortments of compositions can be acquired by utilizing fluctuating measures of the mediums that are utilized in oil artistic creations. The most ordinarily involved mediums in oil painting are linseed oil, sunflower oil and stand oil. The long oil paints are gotten by adding more medium to the oil tones, while in the short oil paints medium is utilized to a base. One significant piece of oil painting is the layering of the tones being utilized on the material. It is recommended that you ought to add meager layers of varieties first and gradually continue adding thicker layers of varieties. You ought to begin painting the greater pieces of your oil painting and afterward continue with adding subtleties to your canvas. The typical strategy that ought to be continued in an oil painting is as per the following: material, arranged gypsum, under-painting, slender paints, thick paints and stain.

Gypsum is utilized for treating the material prior to applying paint on them. It helps the oil tones to stay stayed with the material better than typical. Stain is the material that is added to an oil painting solely after it has dried all around ok. By adding to stain you will actually want to guarantee that your artistic creation remains appropriately kept up with and doesn't get harmed without any problem. Another brief expansion that you can make to your oil painting whenever it has dried is the repair stain. The repair stain that is added to the oil artistic creations can be effortlessly taken out with the assistance of gum turpentine. Having an unmistakable comprehension of these terms and realities will assist you with find out about oil compositions, and you will actually want to concoct preferred nature of canvases over previously. Consider the possibility that I show you how to get everything rolling with drawing and painting no sweat following straightforward advances.

STRAIGHTFORWARD TIPS TO PAINT BETTER WITH OIL PAINTS

The main way to use oil paints in a work of art is you must be ready for the wreck it makes while painting and the time this medium takes for drying. Oils are untidy, and keeping in mind that composition, watch out for your hands, your garments and your studio. You must be ready for oil paints with clothes, additional harsh tissue papers and additional room in your functioning studio. This is exceptionally convenient when you unintentionally drop some or dribble some paint on the floor, or inadvertently on the actual craftsmanship where you don't wish to have it. You must be ready for the time it takes for drying.

Oil paints really do call for a ton of investment to dry so keep void space or a wall to allow your fine arts to dry for the necessary time. Besides, utilizing a decent quality more slender while utilizing oils is significant choosing the right quality and the right amount of oil paint is vital. You can attempt the brush strokes with variety on an edge of the material to comprehend the right required conceal as too slim variety won't be adequate to tie the variety and too thick a medium on brush won't be not difficult to paint and will make an unpleasant surface on your material. An extremely meager medium won't give the ideal impact and may likewise make your specialty look dull in the wake of drying.

The third method for utilizing and painting better with oil paints is to choose a fast drying specialist. A decent quality oil paint drying specialist makes all the difference and decreases the drying time significantly this implies there is less dropping and spilling of endlessly variety dropping mishaps. You likewise finish the craftsmanship quicker. Numerous specialists have hardly any familiarity with these speedy drying specialists that work with drying of oils quicker and diminish the expected time for drying. This method for utilizing a speedy drying specialist is exceptionally useful when you have an arranged commission work and less time, particularly during rainstorm when this medium demands the most investment to dry and furthermore in this season there are chances of your fine art finding organism during the drying system. The fourth way to use oil paints in any work of art is the proper procedure and cycle. While you paint bit by bit utilizing oils, you should constantly make sure in any case utilizing the lighter tones. First go through lighter tones by filling the significant pieces of your material where light tones are required. The framing and subtleties in your work of art should be painted later on. This limits the over lapping of oil paints and you additionally utilize less amount of variety when contrasted with when you paint hazier tones first, where you would go through a greater amount of light variety oil paint nevertheless experience issues in getting the right appearance of the item you are painting. The fifth basic hint to utilize this medium actually is let the layers of paint on your material dry well. This is vital that you permit the base and all the paint layers to get dry well. This tip is particularly useful when you are doing a variety field theoretical craftsmanship piece. You limit the gamble of getting sloppy varieties on your material. Normally when we paint abstracts the interaction is laying of one variety over the other, the craftsmen chooses not many regions that they wish to feature and some that are covered up and over lapped with another variety. Here this tip would be exceptionally useful, generally in the end you might get a sloppy and filthy hued work of art with patches of grimy tans, which might be of no utilization. Oil paints are a generally excellent medium and following specific basic hints you can paint effectively with this medium and make great fine art.

CHAPTER THREE

METHODS PAINTING FOR FLEDGLINGS

Here are some do's and don'ts for oil painting strategies that I've gathered as a beginning rundown for the side interest of painting for fledglings.

ACCOMPLISHES FOR OIL PAINTING

Do cover fat up lean. Fat over incline just implies that the initial not many layers should be applied meagerly. This is done so the layers dry quicker. The quicker dry time keeps the completed the process of painting from "wrinkling". One approach to accomplishing this is to involve more oil in the paint in resulting layers to guarantee they don't dry before the lower layers do. Do utilize water mixable or water-dissolvable oil paint. Water mixable and oil sounds inconsistent however they aren't. These paints don't contain water yet water can be blended in with them. Tidy up of brushes is extraordinarily simple utilizing cleanser and water. Likewise you are not presenting yourself to cruel and hurtful solvents as cleaning supplies. I energetically suggest utilizing water mixable oil paints. Do permit yourself an opportunity to let layers of your composition to dry. Dissimilar to acrylic paint, oil painting requires more persistence and time to finish. Take care of business in layers. Because of the idea of oils, craftsmen need to fabricate layers. It's simpler to do this assuming the principal layer had opportunity and willpower to "dry". You achieve this by applying slender layers in the start of your work.

DON'TS FOR OIL PAINTING

Try not to anticipate that a composition should be finished in hours or brief timeframes. The oil paint gets some margin to dry since it's anything but a basic dissipation process that makes the paint dry. A compound response is occurring and contingent upon what sort of oil you have utilized, it might require days or weeks for parts of the canvas to be sufficiently dry to work. Try not to utilize poisonous or combustible solvents and acetones. Make a point to demand a Material Security Information Sheet or MSDS while purchasing solvents or thinners in the event that you decide to utilize conventional oil paints versus water mixable oils. Recall that even citrus scented thinners can be poisonous and destructive to your wellbeing. A MSDS will portray every one of the dangers related with the item. On the off chance that there is smell or inward breath or actual dangers, for example, combustibility basically buys an unscented or less harmful item. I suggest purchasing water-solvent or water mixable oil paint.

Try not to surrender. Painting is experimentation and loads of training. Continue perusing and contemplating and you will improve your involvement in each concentrate course you complete.

HOW TO MAKE YOUR MOST MEMORABLE REPRESENTATION TO PAINTING

1. Set up the Material

I set up my materials by utilizing white acrylic gesso. I spread a layer of gesso onto the material making the canvas administration smoother with each continuous layer. This fundamental strategy is utilized for oil and acrylic painting. In the event that you are laying out a picture in watercolor you would utilize watercolor paper and consequently this step doesn't make a difference.

2. Get the Sketch of the Photograph or Picture on the Material

There are a few strategies I use to get a precise sketch on a pre-arranged material. The principal strategy I use and educate is the network technique. With the lattice strategy you just put a framework of equivalent squares on both the photograph and the material. Then, at that point, you draw with a pencil what you find in every single square. This makes a line drawing on the material. There are more straightforward techniques however this is the first and once in a while the only one showed in most craftsmanship classes.

3. Pick Your Paint Medium

A paint medium basically implies the kind of paint you are utilizing, oil, acrylic or watercolor for the most part. With oil paint there are a couple of decisions of paint types to utilize. There are conventional oils. These appear to be liked by numerous craftsmen. Customary oil paints require turpentine or different solvents for diminishing and cleaning. You ought to pick unscented solvents because of the unfavorable wellbeing impacts that are conceivable by breathing in poisons tracked down in certain thinners or solvents. Available today are more up to date oil paints called water-solvent or water mixable oil paint. Water mixable paints are not made with water, however can be handily blended in with and cleaned with water making them a lot simpler and wonderful to work with. Acrylic paint is a decent decision of paint in the event that you like a quick drying other option. To hold the paint back from drying to rapidly on the range you just fog or delicately shower the bed now and again. I appreciate working with acrylic paint since I like to see quick outcomes.

Watercolor paint has for some time been a most loved medium among craftsmen. In the event that you appreciate dealing with paper versus material, watercolor is a decent decision for you. Continuous layers of watercolor paint construct ravishing pictures

4. Begin Building Layers of the Representation

With oil paint, you really want to begin lean. You maintain that the base layers should dry quicker than the top thicker layers. For this to happen apply those initial not many layers meagerly. With oil paint it means quite a bit too simply thinks as far as applying brush strokes of variety and afterward rehash. As your representation begins to come to fruition, you can apply thick layers of varieties. With acrylic and watercolor paint, you additionally work in layers. Acrylic paint is added on top and tenderly cleaned in to mix with the lower layers. Watercolor layers are delicately applied until the variety is just about as dim as wanted.

DIFFERENT OIL PAINTING MEDIUMS TO IMPROVE YOUR OIL PICTURE WORKS OF ART

Winsor and Newton Liquin: This low gleam fluid alkyd medium is utilized to work on the progression of oil paint and smooth out any brushwork, it additionally increments straightforwardness making it the ideal vehicle for flimsy coatings and mixing work. Additionally, by smoothing brushwork it is great for better subtleties. Liquin can likewise speed up evaporating by to a portion of the standard time contingent upon the oil tone to medium proportion.

Refined Linseed Oil: Generally blended in with turpentine to make an oil painting medium, refined linseed oil can likewise be utilized all alone. Linseed oil builds the smoothness of paint and furthermore the straightforwardness so again it is an optimal oil mode for dainty coatings and mixing. Hinders drying permitting you to work longer with the paint.

Roberson-Parris Marble Medium: Is produced using refined beeswax, turpentine and an engineered copal stain or dammar tar. Blended in with oil paint at a proportion of 1:3 and weakened with redressed soul of turpentine, this oil medium is utilized to make a non-reflecting matte like surface that can be great for making the deception of profundity, particularly for dull foundations behind a picture.

Range Alkaflow: Range Alkaflow is an alkyd based oil painting medium that is utilized to thin oils and smooth out brush strokes. Its belongings are like Liquin, in spite of the fact that Alkaflow is a touch more gooey and makes a shine like completion. So again it is an oil painting medium ideal for slender coatings anyway the sparkle it makes is greater for regions, for example, the eyes or lips to give the understanding of dampness or sparkle.

Roberson-Coating Medium This oil painting medium is precisely exact thing it says on the jug; an oil medium you blend in with the paint explicitly to make slim coatings. It works on the progression of the paint as is accordingly great for mixing and better definite work too.

THE END